The Little Book of

Christian Rituals in the Home

Tom Gunning

First published 2007 by
Veritas Publications
7/8 Lower Abbey Street
Dublin 1
Ireland
Email publications@veritas.ie
Website www.veritas.ie

10 9 8 7 6 5 4 3 2 1

ISBN 978 1 84730 023 2

Copyright © Tom Gunning, 2007

A catalogue record for this book is available from the British Library.

Scripture quotations are from the *Jerusalem Bible* version of the Scriptures, copyright © 1966, 1967 and 1968 by Darton, Longman Todd Ltd. and Doubleday and Co. Ltd.

'A Celtic Bed Blessing', 'A Celtic Prayer to Mary' and 'An Old Celtic Prayer' are from Douglas Hyde's *The Religious Songs of Connaught*, courtesy of Irish University Press, 1972. 'Old Celtic House Blessing' is from Alexander Carmichael's *Carmina Gadelica*, Vol. III, courtesy of Scottish University Press Ltd., 1976. 'Breaking New Land' and 'A Celtic Prayer of Peace' are from David Adam's *The Edge of Glory: Prayers in the Celtic Tradition*, courtesy of Triangle, 1985. 'A Poem to be Said on Hearing the Birds Sing', translated by Douglas Hyde, is from Padraic Colum's *Anthology of Irish Verse*, courtesy of Boni and Liveright, 1922. 'Stopping by Woods on a Snowy Evening' by Robert Frost is from *Selected Poems*, Penguin, 1973. 'Lament 10' by Jan Kochanowski is from *Laments*, translated by Seamus Heaney, courtesy of Faber & Faber, 1995. 'Mid-Term Break' by Seamus Heaney is from *Death of a Naturalist*, Faber & Faber, 1991. 'And the days are not full enough' by Ezra Pound is from Neil Astley (ed.) *Staying Alive*, Bloodaxe, 2002. 'A Mother's Prayer' is from *A Sacramental People*, Vol. II, by Michael Drumm and Tom Gunning, courtesy of Columba, 2000.

Designed and typeset by Paula Ryan
Printed in the Republic of Ireland by Betaprint, Dublin

Veritas books are printed on paper made from the wood pulp of managed forests. For every tree felled, at least one tree is planted, thereby renewing natural resources.

Contents

For Ali

Easter
A Feast of Rituals

This book about rituals in the home starts with the festival of Easter. The Church prepares for Easter by setting aside a special period of forty days of reflection and penance which we call Lent, from the old English word *lencten*, 'the spring'. It reminds us of the forty days that Jesus spent in the wilderness and the forty years that the Hebrews wandered in the desert of the Sinai Peninsula.

Easter marks the birth of the Christian Church and we celebrate it in our parishes by attending the Easter ceremonies. Don't miss these, especially the Easter Vigil on Holy Saturday night. You will receive many of the sacred objects you will need for your rituals in the home.

The central symbol of the Christian home is the crucifix. It is appropriate that at Easter time a crucifix be placed in the home.

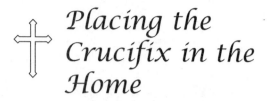

Placing the Crucifix in the Home

The cross is the central symbol of Christianity and it is traditional to place one in the home. It is also the central symbol of Easter and, though it depicts a crucifixion, it has also become a symbol of Christ's victory over death.

A suitable place should be found in the home and young children should be asked where they would like the cross to be placed.

Ritual
You will need a candle, some flowers and some holy water.

Scripture Reading (1 Cor 1:22-25)

And so, while the Jews demand miracles and the Greeks look for wisdom, here we are preaching a crucified Christ; to the Jews an obstacle that they cannot get over, to the pagans madness, but to those who have been called, whether they are Jews or Greeks, a Christ who is the power and wisdom of God. For God's foolishness is wiser than human wisdom, and God's weakness is stronger than human strength.

Lighting the Candle

As the candle is lit the following prayer is said:

We welcome Jesus into our home, into our hearts and into our lives.
May this cross bless our home and be a constant sign of his protection, love and care.

The cross should then be placed on the wall. The candle should be placed close to it and the flowers used to adorn the area.

Blessing

Lord, in our baptism we were marked with the sign of the cross and through this victory we have gained the blessings of eternal life.
May this cross mark our homes with the sign of the King of Peace.
From this moment on, may our home be a place of peace, of love and joy in your presence.

All present bless themselves with the sign of the cross, in the name of the Father and of the Son and of the Holy Spirit.

Shrove Tuesday

Also known as Mardi Gras or Pancake Tuesday, this is the day before Ash Wednesday and was traditionally the day for consuming all the food in the house in preparation for the fasting of Lent. Some families make up pancakes using eggs, flour and milk because in times past people ate no eggs and drank only black tea during Lent. In this way they used all these ingredients before Ash Wednesday.

Before the pancakes are cooked the following prayer is said by all present:

> We thank God for the gift of food and the fruits of the earth.
> We ask you to give us strength through your Holy Spirit as we prepare for this time of Lent.

As the pancakes are being cooked the following text is read. In this piece the prophet Elijah is on his way to Mount Horeb, the Mountain of God. He is tired and hungry as the journey takes him forty days and nights.

Scripture
Reading
(1 Kings
19:1-8)

He himself went on into the desert, a day's journey, and sitting under a furze bush wished he were dead. 'Yahweh,' he said, 'I have had enough. Take my life; I am no better than my ancestors.' Then he lay down and went to sleep. Then all of a sudden an angel touched him and said, 'Get up and eat.' He looked round, and there at his head was a scone baked on hot stones, and a jar of water. He ate and drank and then lay down again. But the angel of Yahweh came back a second time and touched him and said, 'Get up and eat, or the journey will be too long for you.' So he got up and ate and drank, and strengthened by that food he walked for forty days and forty nights until he reached Horeb, God's mountain.

Ritual
As a family, discuss the different things you hope to be able to give up during Lent.

Blessing
Lord, Elijah gave up all food and hope and yet your angels were watching over him to strengthen and take care of him.
Help us to let go of that which is not good and strengthen in this time of letting go.

 Ash Wednesday

Sometimes it is necessary to bring blessed ashes home to those who are sick or unable to leave the home. The following is a ritual for giving ashes to someone at home.

Lighting the Candles

After the candles are lit the following prayer is said by all who are present:

> It is written in the prophet Isaiah: Look, I am going to send my messenger in front of you to prepare your way before you. (Mk 1:2)

Giving of Ashes

As the blessed ashes are placed on the person's head the following is said:

> Repent and believe in the Good News of the Gospel.

Scripture
Reading
(Mk 1:4-8)
John the Baptist was in the desert, proclaiming a baptism of repentance for the forgiveness of sins. All Judaea and all the people of Jerusalem made their way to him, and as they were baptised by him in the river Jordan they confessed their sins. John wore a garment of camel skin, and he lived on locusts and wild honey. In the course of his preaching he said, 'After me is coming someone who is more powerful than me, and I am not fit to kneel down and undo the strap of his sandals. I have baptised you with water, but he will baptise you with the Holy Spirit.'

Blessing

Lord, bless this home and all who live here.
Help us to repent and believe in your word, which is our true nourishment.

Palm Sunday

It is a common custom to bring home some palm after the liturgy of Palm Sunday. It is important to find an appropriate place to put the palm. If you have a sacred place in the home place the palm there during this ritual. Alternatively, the palm can be put behind the cross on the wall.

As the palm is put in the house the following prayer and blessing is said:

Let us adore the Lord as he comes; let us go to meet him with hymns and songs, rejoicing and singing: Blessed be the Lord!

Prayer
Lord, may this palm be a sign that you are welcomed in our home. Protect us always and bless all those who enter our home, stranger, visitor and friend.

Scripture Reading (Jn 12: 12-19)
The next day the great crowd of people who had come up for the festival heard that Jesus was on his way to Jerusalem. They took branches of palm and went out to receive him, shouting: 'Hosanna! Blessed is he who is coming in the name of the Lord, the King of Israel.'

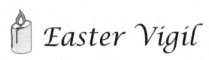 *Easter Vigil*

The Easter Vigil celebrates the resurrection of Jesus from the dead. As a night time celebration it celebrates his resurrection with light, water and fire.

Scripture Reading (Lk 24: 1-50)	But on the first day of the week, at early dawn, they came to the tomb, taking the spices they had prepared. They found the stone rolled away from the tomb, but when they went in, they did not find the body. While they were perplexed about this, suddenly two men in dazzling clothes stood beside them. The women were terrified and bowed their faces to the ground, but the men said to them, 'Why do you look for the living among the dead? He is not here, but has risen.'

Preparation

Tonight is a central celebration in the Christian calendar. At the celebration tonight candles will be used in the ceremony along with water. Make sure to bring some of your own candles and water.

Candles

One of the candles you have brought will be lit from the paschal candle which itself will be lit from the paschal fire in the church. The paschal candle, or Easter candle, is lit during baptisms and funerals. It is in baptism that we receive the gift of eternal life and so the paschal candle reminds us of everlasting life at funerals. After the ceremony is over bring your candles to the priest and ask him to bless them. These candles, which will be used in your home throughout the year, will be a constant symbol of the resurrection, new life and hope. They will be your very own Easter candles.

Water

During the ceremony everyone is blessed with holy water. Water too reminds us of new life and blessings. Bring your own container of water to the ceremony and, along with your candles, ask the priest to bless the water. Like the candles, this blessed and holy water will be a constant symbol of Easter in your home, of hope and new life.

Ritual

When you return home, place the candles in the sacred space, along with the holy water. Light one of the candles and then say the following blessing:

> Lord our God, we rejoice in your resurrection from the dead.
> We rejoice that the darkness of the tomb was replaced by the light of new life.
> Now with these candles and holy water we welcome Easter into our home.
> With this light we welcome life and hope.

Easter Sunday

This is the most significant Sunday in the liturgical year and is marked with a special meal of lamb and wine. In the morning the following prayer can be said:

> Let us wake in the morning filled with your love, and sing and be happy all our days.
> Make our future as happy as our past was sad, the years when we experienced disaster.
> Let your servants see what you can do for them; let their children see your glory; may the sweetness of the Lord be upon us; make all we do succeed. (Ps 90:14-17)

Lighting the Candles Before the Meal

Rejoice! This morning we greet a day like no other! Today a light shines that dispels all darkness. Christ is risen! Alleluia!

Scripture Reading (Is 53: 6-7) We had all gone astray like sheep, each taking his own way, and Yahweh brought the acts of rebellion of all of us to bear on him. Ill-treated and afflicted, he never opened his mouth; like a lamb led to the slaughter-house, like a sheep dumb before its shearers he never opened his mouth.

Out in the Garden

This prayer of praise can be recited out in the garden. It's spring, so look at all the new buds on the trees, all the signs of hope and new life. If there are flowers in the garden pick them for the sacred space (see p. 103).

> From your high halls you water the mountains, satisfying the earth with the fruit of your works.
> For cattle you make the grass grow, and for people the plants they need to bring forth food from the earth, and wine to cheer people's hearts, oil to make their faces glow, bread to make them sturdy of heart.
> (Ps 104:13-15)

Closing Prayer
Place the flowers you have brought in from the garden in the sacred space.

> Lord, may the mystery of Easter fill our lives with hope and gladness.
> May Easter bear fruit in our lives and may we always be children of the light and rise to new life in Christ. Amen.

Holy Water Font

It is traditional in Irish homes to place a holy water font inside the front door or at the kitchen door. Here is a simple ritual to use when putting up your font. It should be placed at a height accessible to children.

Holy water may be obtained from any church or can be blessed by a priest. If it is around Easter time you can use the water which you got blessed at the Easter Holy Vigil.

Scripture Reading (Jn 4:14)

Whoever drinks this water will get thirsty again; but anyone who drinks the water that I shall give will never be thirsty again: the water that I shall give will turn into a spring inside him, welling up to eternal life.

Prayer

Lord, we place this holy water in our home. We pray that as we bless ourselves each day you will protect us and keep us from all harm.

Ritual

Each person then blesses themselves with the holy water saying:

In the name of the Father and of the Son and of the Holy Spirit.

Blessing

May God bless our home and all who live here. May God send his angels now to protect us from all harm.

May God keep us healthy and happy, now, and at all times. Amen.

Using the Holy Water Font

Before a Journey

The person blesses themselves with the holy water. They can then recite the following prayer:

Lord, protect me on the road today as I leave and return to home.

Protect me from danger and help me drive responsibly and carefully.

Send your angels to guide my path and if I break down send me assistance.

Old Irish Prayer
May the road rise to meet you.
May the wind be always at your back.
May the sunshine warm your face.
And the rain fall soft upon your fields.
And until we meet again, may you be held in the palm of God's hand.

Blessing before Going to Work

The person blesses themselves before going to work:

Lord, I give you the work I do today.
Help me to be honest and patient with those
I meet.
Help me to bring calm and happiness to the
workplace.
Help me to endure those who annoy or are
out to get me.
Thank you, for my job and the ability to
work.
May all I do be sown for an eternal harvest.

Blessing before Exams

*The person blesses themselves and then says the
following:*

Lord, there will be many tests in my life but
the exam today is my main concern.
Lord, help me to do my best.
Help my strained memory in times of doubt
and my tired hand write it all down.
Let your will be done and may all I do lead me
to you.

Blessing When a Child Falls and Hurts Themselves

Place some holy water on the sore limb and say:

Lord, we will fall many times in life but today's fall needs immediate attention.
With this holy water, take the pain away and send your angels to heal the little wound.
Feeling better already, make us fit again to play and play until the end of day.

Blessing the House before Bedtime

Each person blesses themselves, saying the following:

Lord, protect our home in the dark hours of the night.
Enfold your loving arms around each sleepy body, heart and soul.
May we dream the happy dreams of God's own beloved children.
And send your angels now to protect our home 'til the sun creeps through the veil of dawn.

A Celtic Bed Blessing

I lie down tonight with Mary and with her Son,
with the Mother of my King who does me protect
from evil-deeds.
I shall not lie with the evil and the evil shall not
lie with me.
But I shall lie with God, and God shall lie along
with me. The right hand of God under my head,
the girdle of the Nine Angels with me
from the top of my head to the skin of my foot-
soles.

Douglas Hyde, *The Religious Songs of Connaught*, p. 31.

Old Celtic House Blessing

May God give blessing
To the house that is here;

May Jesus give blessing
To the house that is here;

May Spirit give blessing
To the house that is here;

My Three give blessing
To the house that is here.

Alexander Carmichael,
Carmina Gadelica, Vol. III, p. 361.

A Morning Blessing

Lord our God, we have awoken from darkness to be children of the light.
Bless our day so at evening time we will find rest in your presence.

Let us wake in the morning filled with your love, and sing and be happy all our days; make our future as happy as our past was sad, the years when we experienced disaster.

Let your servants see what you can do for them.
Let their children see your glory.
May the sweetness of the Lord be upon us.
Make all we do succeed. (Ps 90)

A Poem to be said on Hearing the Birds Sing

A fragrant prayer upon the air
My child taught me,
Awaken there, the morn is fair,
The bird sings free.
Now dawns the day, awake and pray
And bend the knee,
The Lamb who lay beneath the clay
Was slain for thee.

Trans. Douglas Hyde, *Anthology of Irish Verse.*

Sowing &
Planting

The garden with its rhythms of death, growth,
first fruits and new life is a rich symbol of spiritual
life. While working in the garden the following
texts can be used so as to transform your time
there into a spiritual experience. Becoming aware
of the rhythm of nature is a reminder of our own
inner life.

A Time for Life and Death

This text from the book of Ecclesiastes is famous for its insights into life and death. It is an ideal text to help one reflect on the rhythms of nature and life.

> There is a season for everything, a time for every occupation under heaven:
> A time for giving birth, a time for dying;
> a time for planting, a time for uprooting what has been planted.
> A time for killing, a time for healing;
> a time for knocking down, a time for building.
> A time for tears, a time for laughter;
> a time for mourning, a time for dancing.
> A time for throwing stones away, a time for gathering them;
> a time for embracing, a time to refrain from embracing.
> A time for searching, a time for losing;
> a time for keeping, a time for discarding.
> A time for tearing, a time for sewing;
> a time for keeping silent, a time for speaking.
> A time for loving, a time for hating;
> a time for war, a time for peace. (Eccl 3:1-8)

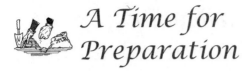

A Time for Preparation

Here is an old Celtic prayer to be said before breaking the ground. Our forebears wrote prayers such as these based on their own deep sense of the presence of God in creation. There was little distinction made between their ordinary working lives and prayer. God was in the midst of all and at all times.

Breaking New Land

All that I dig with the spade I do it with my
Father's aid.
All that I dig with the spade I do it with my
Saviour's aid.
All that I dig with the spade I do with the Spirit's
aid.
All that I dig with the spade I do it in God the
Three's aid.
Each turning of the soil I make I do it for the
Three in One's sake.

David Adam, *The Edge of Glory: Prayers in the Celtic Tradition*, p. 29.

Cast your Worries Aside in the Garden

Based on God's creative works, Jesus tells the following story of divine care and providence. Go into your garden. Sit down, listen, smell and see. Then read the following text:

Scripture Reading (Lk 12: 22-28)

Then he said to his disciples, 'That is why I am telling you not to worry about your life and what you are to eat, nor about your body and how you are to clothe it. For life is more than food, and the body more than clothing. Think of the ravens. They do not sow or reap; they have no storehouses and no barns; yet God feeds them. And how much more you are worth than the birds! Can any of you, however much you worry, add a single cubit to your span of life? If a very small thing is beyond your powers, why worry about the rest? Think how the flowers grow; they never have to spin or weave; yet, I assure you, not even Solomon in all his royal robes was clothed like one of them. Now if that is how God clothes a flower which is growing wild today and is thrown into the furnace tomorrow, how much more will he look after you, who have so little faith!'

A Time for Enriching the Soil and Sowing

Each year the soil in the garden needs to be enriched with fertiliser. Before the soil is enriched for sowing and to provide for a good harvest, this is the time to think about how we ourselves are in constant need of spiritual enrichment.

The following scripture passage tells us how we are asked to receive the word of God like good soil so that it can reap a rich harvest in our lives.

The Sower

Scripture Reading (Mt 13: 4-9)

As he sowed, some seeds fell on the edge edge of the path, and the birds came and ate them up. Others fell on patches of rock where they found little soil and sprang up at once, because there was no depth of earth; but as soon as the sun came up they were scorched and, not having any roots, they withered away. Others fell among thorns, and the thorns grew up and choked them. Others fell on rich soil and produced their crop, some a hundredfold, some sixty, some thirty. Anyone who has ears should listen

Seeds that need to be sowed can then be planted in the ground. Little children love sowing seeds and should be encouraged to plant the seeds and cover them over. The following prayer can be said for all the plants and seeds in the garden:

Lord, visit this land with your bounty, life and goodness.
May this soil and the seeds we have sown reap us a rich harvest for our home and continue to sow in our own hearts the seeds of your love.

A Time for God's Bounty

This psalm could be read before watering the ground and reminds us, not only in the land but also in our lives, that 'abundance flows wherever you pass'.

You visit the earth and water it,
You load it with riches;
God's rivers brim with water,
To provide their grain.

This is how you provide it:
by drenching its furrows, by levelling its ridges, by softening it with showers, by blessing the first fruits.
You crown the year with your bounty,
Abundance flows wherever you pass;
The desert pastures overflow,
The hillsides are wrapped in joy,
The meadows are dressed in flocks,
The valleys are clothed in wheat,
What shouts of joy, what singing! (Ps 65:9-13)

A Time for Harvest

This is a psalm of praise to God who shows kindness to us and whose face smiles upon us. Having sown the seeds it is time for harvest, for God has blessed us.

May God show kindness and bless us, and make his face shine on us!
Then the earth will acknowledge your ways, and all nations your power to save.

Let the nations praise you, O God, Let all the nations praise you!

Let the nations rejoice and sing for joy, for you judge the world with justice.
You judge the peoples with fairness, you guide the nations on earth.
Let the nations praise you, God, let all the nations praise you.
The earth has yielded its produce; God, our God has blessed us.
May God continue to bless us, and be revered to the very ends of the earth. (Ps 67)

 *The May Altar*

It is traditional in Irish homes to create a sacred place for Mary during the month of May. Flowers are brought in from the garden and placed before a statue of Mary somewhere in the home. Sometimes children like to place the May Altar in their home. Bluebells are a flower in bloom in May and are often used.

Placing the flowers before the statue, pray:

> Hail Mary, full of grace
> The Lord is with thee.
> Blessed art thou among women,
> And blessed is the fruit of thy womb, Jesus.
>
> Holy Mary, Mother of God.
> Pray for us sinners,
> Now and at the hour of our death.
> Amen.

Scripture Reading (Lk 1: 46-49)

And Mary said: My soul proclaims the greatness of the Lord and my spirit rejoices in God my Saviour; because he has looked upon the humiliation of his servant. Yes, from now onwards all generations will call me blessed, for the Almighty has done great things for me. Holy is his name.

A Celtic Prayer to Mary
All hail to thee, Mary
With grace from above.
And all Hail to thee, Queen,
Who comest in love,
And blessed thou art
Amongst women, and blest
Is thy holy child, Jesus,
Who lay on thy breast.
The Religious Songs of Connaught, p. 393.

 # Winter Solstice

In modern times we have become less connected with the rhythms of nature and the seasons, yet our forebears marked such passages and changes with precision. For them, there was a clear connection between growth, planting and life itself. If the crops failed, as the famine showed, people died. For our ancestors there was a clear connection between life and the power of the sun to bring forth produce from the earth. In the Celtic year, along with the four solar festivals there were also the four agricultural festivals of *Imbolg* (winter), *Bealtaine* (spring), *Lughnasa* (summer) and *Samhain* (autumn). Together, all these festivals celebrated the abundance and bounty of the earth and the natural world.

The winter solstice marks the shortest day of the year. On the 21 December the following morning prayer is said:

Opening Prayer

We are a people baptised into the light of Christ, praised be the name of the Lord.

Let Every Creature Praise the Lord

Bless the Lord, all the Lord's creation: praise and glorify him forever!

Bless the Lord, angels of the Lord, praise and glorify him forever!

Bless the Lord, heavens, praise and glorify him forever!

Bless the Lord, all the waters above the heavens, praise and glorify him forever!

Bless the Lord, powers of the Lord, praise and glorify him forever!

Bless the Lord, sun and moon, praise and glorify him forever!

Bless the Lord, stars of heaven, praise and glorify him forever!

Bless the Lord, all rain and dew, praise and glorify him forever!

Bless the Lord, every wind, praise and glorify him forever!

Bless the Lord, fire and heat, praise and glorify him forever!

Bless the Lord, cold and warmth, praise and glorify him forever!

Bless the Lord, dew and snow-storm, praise and glorify him for ever!

Bless the Lord, frost and cold, praise and glorify him forever!

Bless the Lord, ice and snow, praise and glorify him forever!

Bless the Lord, nights and days, praise and glorify him forever!
Bless the Lord, light and darkness, praise and glorify him forever!
Bless the Lord, lightning and cloud, praise and glorify him forever!
Let the earth bless the Lord: praise and glorify him forever! (Ps 3:57-73)

Scripture Reading (Jn 1:5-7) This is what we have heard from him and are declaring to you: God is light, and there is no darkness in him at all. If we say that we share in God's life while we are living in darkness, we are lying, because we are not living the truth. But if we live in light, as he is in light, we have a share in another's life, and the blood of Jesus, his Son, cleanses us from all sin.

The following poem by Robert Frost is one of the most famous and memorable pieces of verse in the English language. It is a haunting poem set during the winter solstice, 'the darkest evening of the year'.

Stopping by Woods on a Snowy Evening
Whose woods these are I think I know
His house is in the village, though;
He will not see me stopping here
To watch his woods fill up with snow.

My little horse must think it queer
To stop without a farmhouse near
Between the woods and frozen lake
The darkest evening of the year.

He gives his harness bells a shake
To ask if there is some mistake.
The only other sound's the sweep
Of easy wind and downy flake.

The woods are lovely, dark and deep,
But I have promises to keep,
And miles to go before I sleep,
And miles to go before I sleep.
Selected Poems, p. 130.

Closing Prayer

Lord our God, we have awoken from darkness
to be children of the light.
Enlighten our hearts and minds so that we
may follow your path.

Spring Equinox

Today on the equator there is equal day and night. The following morning prayer is said:

Opening Prayer

Blessed be God the creator of the heavens and the earth, of the lands and the sea, of day and night.

Blessed be God who made the mountains and the rivers, the forests and the lakes, the sun and the stars.

Alleluia!

Praise the Lord from the heavens, praise him in the heights.
Praise him, all his angels, praise him, all his host.
Praise him, sun and moon, praise him, shining stars.
Praise him, highest heavens and the waters above the heavens.
Let them praise the name of the Lord. (Ps 148:1-5)

Scripture
Reading
(Gen 1:
1-5)

In the beginning God created heaven and earth. Now the earth was a formless void, there was darkness over the deep, with a divine wind sweeping over the waters. God said, 'Let there be light,' and there was light. God saw that light was good, and God divided light from darkness. God called light 'day' and darkness he called 'night'. Evening came and morning came: the first day.

Closing Prayer

Lord our God,

We have awoken from darkness to be children of the light.

Bless our day so at evening time we will find rest in your presence.

Summer Solstice

June 21 is the longest day of the year. The following evening prayer is said as the sun sets on this day:

Opening Prayer

Christ, you are the light of the world, the day star that dispels all darkness. May we never live in the land of shadow.

Scripture Reading (Eccl 1: 4-11)

A generation goes, a generation comes, yet the earth stands firm forever. The sun rises, the sun sets; then to its place it speeds and there it rises. Southward goes the wind, then turns to the north; it turns and turns again; back then to its circling goes the wind. Into the sea all the rivers go, and yet the sea is never filled, and still to their goal the rivers go. All things are wearisome. No man can say that eyes have not had enough of seeing, ears their fill of hearing. What was will be again; what has been done will be done again; and there is nothing new under the sun. Take anything of which it may be said, 'Look now, this is new'. Already, long before our time, it existed. Only no memory remains of earlier times, just as in times to come next year itself will not be remembered.

Closing Prayer

Lord, at the evening of this day we offer you the work we have done.

May we always find rest in your presence as we thank you for the gift of light and the wonders of creation. Amen.

 Autumn Equinox

On 21 September there is equal day and night at the equator. The following morning prayer is said:

Opening Prayer

Let all the nations of the earth praise the name of the Lord. Praise the Lord who created the heavens and the earth, the sun and the stars, the night and the light.

O God, be gracious and bless us and let your face shed its light upon us.
So will your ways be known upon earth and all nations learn your saving help.

Let the peoples praise you, O God; let all the peoples praise you.

Let the nations be glad and exult, for you rule the world with justice.
With fairness you rule the peoples, you guide the nations on earth.

Let the peoples praise you, O God; let all the peoples praise you. (Ps 67:1-5)

Scripture Reading (Lk 1: 76-79)

And you, little child, you shall be called Prophet of the Most High, for you will go before the Lord to prepare a way for him. To give his people knowledge of salvation through the forgiveness of their sins; this by the tender mercy of our God who from on high will bring the rising Sun to visit us, to give light to those who live in darkness and the shadow of death, and to guide our feet into the way of peace.

Closing Prayer

Lord our God,

We have awoken from darkness to be children of the light.

Bless our day so at evening time we will find rest in your presence.

Lighting Candles

Have you ever sat outside on a summer's evening around a fire? There's something about it. Sharing stories with friends as the sun sets. Our forebears were doing the same thousands of years ago. Sitting around open fires. And most probably in a thousand years time, people will still sit around open fires as light fades into dark.

Fire is one of the most ancient of Christian symbols and for generations people have been lighting candles in their homes to mark special events. Here are some suggestions for lighting candles in the home to mark a special time.

 # *Sickness*

Sickness is that one reality that can force us out to the very edges of human experience. At such times we need to get strength and comfort from the Christian community.

Here is a ritual which can be used by a lay person in the home when someone is sick:

Lighting Candles

As the candles in the room are lit the following prayer of blessing is said:

Jesus, you are the light of the world.
Bless these candles and make them a sign of our hope in you.

Scripture	The people that walked in darkness
Reading	have seen a great light;
(Is 9:1-2)	on those who live in a land of deep
	shadow a light has shone.
	You have made their gladness greater,
	you have made their joy increase;
	They rejoice in your presence as men
	rejoice at harvest time,
	as men are happy when they are
	dividing the spoils.

Placing the Cross at the Bedside

As the cross is placed near the bedside the following text can be read:

Scripture Reading (Eph 3: 20-21)	Glory be to him whose power, working in us, can do infinitely more than we can ask or imagine; glory be to him from generation to generation in the Church and in Christ Jesus, for ever and ever. Amen.

Holy Water

All present bless themselves with holy water, saying:

In the name of the Father and of the Son and of the Holy Spirit. Amen.

Laying on of Hands

From the earliest church the laying on of hands has been a sign of blessing and healing. First a family member reads the following text from the Gospel of Matthew:

After he had come down from the mountain large crowds followed him. Suddenly a man with a virulent skin-disease came up and bowed low in front of him, saying, 'Lord, if you are willing, you can cleanse me.' Jesus stretched out his hand and touched him, saying, 'I am willing. Be cleansed.' And his skin disease was cleansed at once. (Mt 8:1-4)

Those gathered then place their hands upon the sick person, on the head or shoulders. As they do so they say the following prayer:

N., we pray for you.
May the God of love and kindness heal you from sickness and comfort you in your distress.

May God's Spirit strengthen you in weakness and give you life and health to ease your suffering and release your pain.

And may you find hope in Christ who rose from the tomb and conquered death.
May he now heal you in body, mind and soul
And bring you everlasting peace.

Lord, you raised the dead, gave sight to the blind, made the lame walk and the deaf hear.

Listen to our prayer in this time of need and visit N. with your healing presence.

Take N. into your loving and healing embrace. Dispel all worry and fear and fill them with your wholeness and wellbeing. Amen.

Closing Prayer
Our Father,
Who art in Heaven,
Hallowed be thy name.
Thy Kingdom come,
Thy will be done,
On earth as it is in heaven.
Give us this day our daily bread,
And forgive us our trespasses,
As we forgive those who trespass against us,
And lead us not into temptation,
But deliver us from evil. Amen.

Other Occasions to Light Candles

A Time of Worry

Lord, you remember those you left in the upper room full of despair, worry and fear.

You sent your spirit with tongues of fire, lightening the darkness in the hearts of men and women.

Visit me now and send your spirit to dispel the darkness that is overcoming my weary and anxious heart.

Lord, let this candle be a sign of your presence. Lift the darkness and take unto you that which is troubling me now.

A Celtic Prayer of Peace
Deep peace of the running wave to you
Deep peace of the flowing air to you
Deep peace of the quiet earth to you
Deep peace of the shining stars to you
Deep peace of the Son of Peace to you.

The Iona Community, from *The Edge of Glory*, p. 91.

Remembering the Dead

A special candle could be lit in front of a favourite picture of the deceased.

We remember now N. who died x years ago. Though time has passed it has been shadowed by your absence.

Though our lives continue on we still remember your face, voice, laughter and presence in our home.

We light this candle as an enduring sign of your presence in our memory and in our hearts.

We pray that the angels have led you to the outstretched arms of your loving Father in heaven.

As this light shines so too your memory dispels the darkness of absence.
Until we meet again, be happy, N., in your just reward.

Someone Travelling a Long Distance Home

We pray for N. who is travelling
a long distance to visit our home and stay with
us tonight.

Lord, protect our visitor
as they travel over sea and land.
Send your angels to guard and protect a
pathway to our home.

God's speed to the weary traveller
as we look forward to   stories, embraces,
laugher and tears.

Teenager Going out for the Night

Though it saddens us to let them go,
we know our young must leave the nesting
safety of our home.

Lord, please protect our child as they spread
their wings tonight to socialise, laugh and play.

Keep them safe from harm.
Give them your wisdom and understanding
and the gift of courage and right judgement.

Prayer of Confirmation

Send your Holy Spirit upon them to be their helper and guide.

Give them the spirit of wisdom and understanding, the spirit of right judgement and courage,

the spirit of knowledge and reverence.

Fill them with the spirit of wonder and awe in your presence.

We ask this, through Christ our Lord. Amen.

Prayer to the Holy Spirit

Come Holy Spirit, fill the hearts of your faithful and kindle in them the fire of your love.

Send forth your Spirit and they shall be created, and you shall renew the face of the earth.

Pregnancy &

Childbirth

Thus says Yahweh who made you,
Who formed you from the womb, who is
your help. (Is 44:2)

 # Pregnancy

The preparations for birth are amongst the most sacred actions we can ever experience as we prepare for the gift of life. It is important to recognise this sacred time for what it is as we prepare clothes, prams and nurseries in gladness and anticipation. Here are some texts that could be used at various times during pregnancy.

Blessing the Nursery

Blessings are a share in the gift of God's promise and love for us. This blessing could be said just after the nursery has been prepared.

We call you, little child, into this world, as we prepare a place for you in our home; there is a room prepared with pictures, toys and clothes. There's a little bath and a tiny bed, small chairs, tables and a new pram.

With watchful care God forms you and with immeasurable love we wait for you.
We ask God to bless every tiny part that grows and stretches and forms.

May you be bright and cheerful and happy and as strong and healthy as you can be.

Scripture
Reading
(Mk 10:
13-160)

People were bringing little children to him, for him to touch them. The disciples turned them away, but when Jesus saw this he was indignant and said to them, 'Let the little children come to me; do not stop them; for it is to such as these that the Kingdom belongs. I tell you most solemnly, anyone who does not welcome the Kingdom of God like a little child will never enter it.' Then he put his arms around them, laid his hands on them and gave them his blessing.

Prayer before Giving Birth

As dawn dispels night so light overcomes the lurking shadows of fear and worry. Candles have always been sacred symbols of protection and hope. A candle is lit in the home during the difficult time of childbirth. The following prayer could then be said:

In our advent, we have waited for you, little child, to leave the darkness of the womb and enter the light of our embrace.

With expectant hearts we ask our Father to bless the work of the midwives and doctors and the work of their human hands.

In the light of hope may God bless our mother. Strengthen her body and soul and restore her to full health. Amen.

It was you who drew me from the womb
and soothed me on my mother's breast.
On you was I cast from my birth,
from the womb I have belonged to you.
(Ps 22:9-10)

Crossing the Threshold

A moment that can go unnoticed is when a new infant is brought into the home for the first time. Just as the new child is brought across the threshold the following prayer could be said:

We welcome you little child into our home, across the threshold and into the place prepared for you.
May you find health and happiness here and may you be safe and warm in our embrace.

We thank God for the blessing that you are
and may you be happy with us
all the days of our lives.

Scripture
Reading
(Ps 71:
5-6)

For you alone are my hope, Lord, Yahweh I have trusted you since my youth, I have relied on you since I was born. You have been my potion since my mother's womb and the constant theme of my praise.

Placing a Cross in the Nursery

When the child comes home a cross and flowers could be placed in the nursery. The following prayer could be used:

May God send his angels to protect you, little one, and may his face shine on you both day and night.

Let us praise and thank the Lord for you, little child, and the gift that you are, and may you be safe here now and all your days.

Night Feed

The night feed is a special time for parents to be with their child. It is a time of strengthening and growth. Here is a little ritual to be used during the feed based on the ancient Christian practice of placing the sign of the cross on the newly born.

Trace the sign of the cross on the child's forehead
    May God strengthen your mind and
    may you be full of wisdom and insight.

Trace the sign of the cross on the child's throat
    May the spirit of God's own creativity
    dwell in you and your unique little self.

Trace the sign of the cross on the child's chest
    May your heart be healthy and bursting with
    love and may God's own spirit dwell in your
    little soul.

Guardian Angel Prayer
Angel of God, my Guardian dear
to whom God's love commits me here.
Ever this day be at my side
to light and guard and rule and guide. Amen.

Scripture Reading (Eph 3: 16-19) Out of his infinite glory, may he give you the power through his Spirit for your hidden self to grow strong, so that Christ may live in your hearts through faith, and then, planted in love and built on love, you will with all the saints have strength to grasp the breadth and the length, the height and the depth; until, knowing the love of Christ, which is beyond all knowledge, you are filled with the utter fullness of God.

Burning Oils

Oil is an ancient symbol in the Christian tradition. In the West it was often seen as a source of strengthening, whereas in the East it was seen as a symbol of the presence of God. Often oils used in sacraments are scented with balsam and those anointed are fragrant with the presence of Christ. Lately people have taken scented oils into their homes to be used in oil burners. Here are some prayers and texts that can be used when burning oils.

Bath Time

Lord, you take away burdens that are heavy
to bear.
You bring healing to tired limbs, weariness
and pain.

Restore my body, mind and soul in the
warm and relaxing waters of my treasured
bath time.

May the perfume of this oil cover me like a
healing balm, soothing me into the joy of
your divine presence.

Let me breathe in the loveliness of the Lord
and so tonight sleep the sleep of angels.

An Old Celtic Prayer
A messenger from God before me,
An angel of God above my head,
The oil of Christ upon my body
And God before me where I am led.
The Religious Songs of Connaught, p. 255.

Entering a New Home

All is strange in the new home, as its empty and hollow sound echoes in every room.

We burn this oil now, familiar in its scent of our old home and things wished and longed for.

As this perfume spreads throughout our new home, may your presence, Lord, fill every room and space and place.

Lord, dispel all darkness from this house and fill our new home with your joy, blessing and comforting presence.

A Celtic House Blessing
God give grace
To this dwelling place.

Christ give grace
To this dwelling place.

Spirit give grace
To this dwelling place.

The Whole Family is Home Safe

Slowly the house fills with each returning footstep, and familiar sounds envelop the emptiness of each room.

The whole family is home safe to eat and sleep, once again in our loving care.

We thank you Lord for the gift of our family returned.
And so we burn this oil to remind us of your enduring presence.

The whole family returned.

Remembering the Dead

Lament 10
O presence missed,
Comfort me, haunt me; you whom I have lost,
Come back again, be shadow, dream, or ghost.
Jan Kochanowski, *Laments.*

In baptism we are given the gift of everlasting life and enshrined in Christian faith is the belief that after death we enjoy eternal life. The following are some suggestions as to how we can remember our dead in ritual, word and symbol.

Mid-Term Break

I sat all morning in the college sick bay
Counting bells knelling classes to a close,
At two o'clock our neighbors drove me home.

In the porch I met my father crying –
He had always taken funerals in his stride –
And Big Jim Evans saying it was a hard blow.

The baby cooed and laughed and rocked the pram
When I came in, and I was embarrassed
By old men standing up to shake my hand

And tell me they were 'sorry for my trouble,'
Whispers informed strangers I was the eldest,
Away at school, as my mother held my hand

In hers and coughed out angry tearless sighs.
At ten o'clock the ambulance arrived
With the corpse, stanched and bandaged by the nurses.

Next morning I went up into the room.
Snowdrops and candles soothed the bedside; I saw him
For the first time in six weeks. Paler now,

Wearing a poppy bruise on the left temple,
He lay in the four foot box as in a cot.
No gaudy scars, the bumper knocked him clear.

A four foot box, a foot for every year.
Seamus Heaney, *Death of a Naturalist*, p. 15.

 Planting

Snowdrops soothed the bedside of the dead child in Seamus Heaney's poem and it reminds us that after the death of autumn, bulbs promise life next spring. What appears to be dead will rise again. Once something is planted we can revisit it and see how it grows and this can remind us how someone who has left us is alive with Christ. A person's favourite plant could be chosen, or perhaps their favourite place in the garden.

Opening Prayer

Let us wake in the morning filled with your love and sing and be happy all our days; make our future as happy as our past was sad.

As the tree or flower is being planted the following Old Celtic prayer is said:

May not more numerous be
The grains of sand by the sea,
Or the blades of grass by the lea
Or the drops of dew on a tree,
Than the blessings upon thy soul
And the souls of the dead with thee
And my soul when life shall flee.

Scripture Reading (Rev 21: 1-4)

Then I saw a new heaven and a new earth; the first heaven and the first earth had disappeared now, and there was no longer any sea. I saw the holy city, and the new Jerusalem, coming down from God out of heaven, as beautiful as a bride all dressed for her husband. Then I heard a loud voice call from the throne, 'You see this city? Here God lives among men. He will make his home among them; they shall be his people, and he will be their God; his name is God-with-them. He will wipe away all tears from their eyes; there will be no more death, and no more mourning or sadness. The world of the past has gone.'

And the days are not full enough
And the days are not full enough
And the nights are not full enough
And life slips by like a field mouse
Not shaking the grass.
Ezra Pound, *Staying Alive*, p. 130.

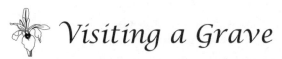 # *Visiting a Grave*

If a family are visiting a grave soon after the death of a loved one or on a first anniversary it will obviously be a difficult moment. The following texts could help the family or relatives express their feelings.

Opening Prayer
Come to me all you who are weary and find life burdensome, and I will refresh you.

The following reflection can be read by different readers:

Reader 1
God our Father,
As we gather by this graveside we remember that you are compassionate and caring.
Comfort us now in our sorrow and loss.
Because we have loved N. so much in life
We now miss him/her in death.

Reader 2
We gather here to pray for N.
Lord Jesus, you overcame darkness and
by dying for us you conquered death
and by rising again you restored life.
In baptism you gave N. the gift of eternal life.

Reader 3

> Help us Lord in our grief
> To hope in life after death
> To believe in everlasting happiness
> To love each other as N. loved us
> To always pray for those who have died
> And always remember the promise of eternal life.

At this point some holy water could be sprinkled over the grave and each person present could bless themselves, saying:

> May God comfort us in death and grant N. eternal life. In the name of the Father and of the Son and of the Holy Spirit. Amen.

Scripture Reading (Jn 11:26)	I am the Resurrection. If anyone believes in me, even though he dies he will live, and whoever lives and believes in me will never die. Do you believe this?

Visiting the Grave at Other Times

November 2 or All Souls Day is the day which the Church has traditionally set aside to remember the dead. The following texts could be used by a graveside whenever one wishes to visit it.

Reader 1

I am the resurrection and the life.

Those who believe in me will live even if they die, and every living person who puts his faith in me will never suffer eternal death.

Reader 2

N., in our hope we see you amongst the angels of heaven and in our faith we believe you enjoy everlasting life. In our love we continue to remember you in thanksgiving and praise.

Reader 1

Yahweh is my shepherd,

I lack nothing. (Ps 23)

At this point some holy water could be sprinkled over the grave and each person present could bless themselves.

> We received the gift of everlasting life in the waters of our baptism.
> In the name of the Father and of the Son and of the Holy Spirit. Amen.

To conclude, all those who have died could be remembered in these prayers of the faithful:

Reader 1

> We pray for our deceased relatives and friends and all who have been good to us as we have journeyed through life. May God grant them the blessings of eternal life.

> R. Lord, hear our prayer.

Reader 2

> We pray for all who have died in the hope of rising again; welcome them, Lord, into the light of you presence.

> R. Lord, hear our prayer.

Closing Prayer

Our Father,
Who art in Heaven,
Hallowed be thy name.
Thy Kingdom come,
Thy will be done,
On earth as it is in heaven.
Give us this day our daily bread,
And forgive us our trespasses,
As we forgive those who trespass against us,
And lead us not into temptation,
But deliver us from evil. Amen.

Visiting the Grave of a Young Child

Facing up to the death of a young child can be one of the most difficult situations. Because of the nature of this bereavement families often make the grave of a child special and other children will often want to bring little toys and teddy bears to the grave. Sometimes people will plant a little garden on a child's grave with snowdrops and other bulbs that will flower in spring.

Opening Prayer

Jesus said: 'Let the children come to me. Do not keep them from me. The Kingdom of God belongs to such as these.' (Mk 10:14)

The following texts could be used by a child's grave soon after death or on a first anniversary.

Lord our God, we gather here in the darkness of sorrow and the silence of loss.

We cannot hope to understand the wisdom of your ways, yet comfort us in the death of one so young.

Grant us faith in your promise that N. may enjoy eternal life with the angels of heaven and the saints of the eternal city.

Parents could be encouraged to compose their own reflections for times like this. The following is an example that could be used:

A Mother's Prayer
The land of our promise was populated with every kind of hope for you,
every kind of wish for your life.
We had imagined who you would be like;
handsome and witty thought your father,
practical and purposeful like your mother I claimed.
Little child why did you go away
before you had learned to live at all?

They said you'd keep us up all night,
that things would never be the same again.
Friends hoped to see your father
with a nappy in his hand,
with tired eyes and a sleepy head.
The fun we'd have putting you to bed.
Little child you have turned our world upside down.

Our tired eyes and our sleepy heads.
Your father enthused about the talents
on his side of the family,
you'd be a professional, a doctor most likely!
I wondered what your ways would be like;
would you be grumpy like your grandfather
or mellow and secretive like grandma?
The questions and questions that go round in my
mind.

You are a mystery and a feast of answers,
an unknown martyr, and an innocent victim
of the dark and terrible ways of this world.
One day this veil of mourning will be lifted
and we will be with you
where you are now going.
Be there N. to put your arms round us,
for in you, little child, we have seen a glimpse of
heaven.
A Sacramental People, p. 155.

At this point some holy water could be sprinkled over the grave and each person present could bless themselves.

Closing Prayer

May the love of God and the peace of the Lord Jesus Christ bless and console us and gently wipe every tear from our eyes.

In the name of the Father and of the Son and of the Holy Spirit. Amen.

Advent

During Advent the Church community waits for the coming of Christ into the world. There are a few reasons why we celebrate the birth of Christ on 25 December. This date is located close to the winter solstice and shortest day of the year on 21 December. So we celebrate the coming of Christ into the world at the darkest time of the year. Also, in the third century when scholars were trying to date Christ's birth based on the solstices they arrived at the 25 December.

Whatever the reason for the date of Christ's birth this was always a sacred time in the cosmic year. The following rituals and prayers are intended to help a family to celebrate the story of Christmas.

The Crèche or Crib

According to tradition, St Francis of Assisi was concerned that some of the local villagers who were unable to read did not know the story of Jesus' birth. So he decided to build a real stable at the back of his church and in it he put live animals and then asked local children to act out the parts of Mary and Joseph. Today, many families put up small cribs in their homes.

Ritual

The family gathers around the crib. All the figures are in the crib except the infant Jesus and the lights have not yet been switched on. Everybody says the opening prayer:

Listen, I bring you news of great joy, a joy to be shared by the whole people. Today in the town of David a saviour has been born to you; he is Christ the Lord.

Scripture Reading (Luke 2: 6-11)

Now it happened that, while they were there, the time came for her to have her child, and she gave birth to a son, her first-born. She wrapped him in swaddling clothes and laid him in a manger because there was no room for them in the living space. In the countryside close by there were shepherds out in the fields keeping guard over their sheep during the watches of the night. An angel of the Lord stood over them and the glory of the Lord shone round them. They were terrified, but the angel said, 'Do not be afraid. Look, I bring you news of great joy, a joy to be shared by the whole people. Today in the town of David a Saviour has been born to you; he is Christ the Lord.'

After this reading the figure of the infant Jesus is put in the crib by the youngest member of the family, who says:

Glory to God in the highest heaven
and peace to all who enjoy God's favour.

Switching on the Lights

As the light is switched on in the crib all genuflect and say:

Emmanuel! God is with us!

Blessing
The eldest member of the family then reads the following blessing:

May God bless this crib and make it a source of hope and joy in our home.

Closing Prayer
Hail Mary, full of grace,
The Lord is with thee.
Blessed art thou among women,
And blessed is the fruit of thy womb, Jesus.

Holy Mary, Mother of God.
Pray for us sinners,
Now and at the hour of our death. Amen.

The Christmas Tree

After the tree has been put up in the house the following rituals are used:

Placing the Star on the Tree

A star can easily be made out of cardboard and tinfoil. Before it is placed on the top of the tree the following text is read:

Scripture Reading (Mt 2:1-8)

After Jesus had been born at Bethlehem in Judaea during the reign of King Herod, suddenly some wise men came to Jerusalem from the east, asking, 'Where is the infant king of the Jews? We saw his star as it rose and have come to do him homage.' When King Herod heard this he was perturbed, and so was the whole of Jerusalem. He called together all the chief priests and the scribes of the people, and enquired of them where the Christ was to be born. They told him, 'At Bethlehem in Judaea, for this is what the prophet wrote: And you, Bethlehem, in the land of Judah, you are by no means the least among the leaders of Judah, for from you will come a leader who will shepherd my people Israel.' Then Herod summoned the wise men to see him privately. He asked them the exact date on which the star had appeared and sent them on to Bethlehem with the words, 'Go and find out all about the child, and when you have found him, let me know, so that I too may go and do him homage'.

Placing Gifts around the Tree

The presents, which the family has bought for each other, are put at the base of the tree. Alternatively, small presents can be hung on the tree. Before this is done the following text is read:

Scripture Reading (Mt 2: 9-12) Having listened to what the king had to say, they set out. And suddenly the star they had seen rising went forward and halted over the place where the child was. The sight of the star filled them with delight, and going into the house they saw the child with his mother Mary, and falling to their knees they did him homage. Then, opening their treasures, they offered him gifts of gold and frankincense and myrrh.

Placing Angels on the Tree

Angels figure at various occasions in the story of the birth of Jesus to guide and protect. Small figures of angels are put on the tree after the following text is read:

Scripture Reading (Mt 2: 13-15)

After the three wise men had left, suddenly the angel of the Lord appeared to Joseph in a dream and said, 'Get up, take the child and his mother with you, and escape into Egypt, and stay there until I tell you, because Herod intends to search for the child and do away with him.' So Joseph got up and, taking the child and his mother with him, left that night for Egypt, where he stayed until Herod was dead. This was to fulfil what the Lord had spoken through the prophet: I called my son out of Egypt.

Putting Tinsel on the Tree

Before the tree is decorated with tinsel the following story could be told:

An angel appeared to Joseph in a dream and told him to go to Egypt because Herod intended to kill all the first born males. And so Joseph took his family and they began to flee into Egypt but soon the soldiers began to catch up on the family and then an angel appeared to Joseph and told him to go into a cave and wait there. They went in fearing the worst but a great spider spun a web over the mouth of the cave. When the soldier came to check the cave he did not go in, presuming nobody was inside. Exhausted, they fell asleep.

In the morning they awoke and the morning sun poured in through the opening of the cave and its rays glistened on the dew that had fallen on the spider's web. They thanked God for having protected them from death.

Switching on the Lights

Most Christmas trees are decorated with electric lights and after they are switched on all gathered could read this final prayer:

Lord, you sent us your son, Jesus.
How faithful and enduring is your love!

Let this evergreen tree remind us
that God is always with us, Emmanuel!

Lord, bless this house tonight and always for
the people who walked in darkness have seen
a great light!

 Christmas Eve

On Christmas Eve a lighted candle is placed in a window. This is an old tradition which is still continued in some homes. The following text is used before the candle is lit and placed in the window:

Prayer

Tonight, we await the coming of Christ into the world.
May this lighted candle welcome Christ into our home.

We remember how the Holy Family were denied a home this night.
May the Light of the World help all those who are without a home tonight.

Scripture Reading (Is 9:1-2)

The people that walked in darkness have seen a great light; on the inhabitants of a country in shadow dark as death light has blazed forth. You have enlarged the nation, you have increased its joy; they rejoice before you as people rejoice at harvest time, as they exult when they are dividing the spoils.

A House Blessing

In an old tradition a parent in the house brings a lighted candle into each room on Christmas Eve. After the lights are put out the following short text could be used before the candle is brought into each room:

Scripture Reading (Is 7:14)

The Lord will give you a sign in any case: it is this: the young woman is with child and will give birth to a son whom she will call Emmanuel.

It was then traditional for the mother of the house to bless everyone present with holy water. After this the following old Celtic prayer was said:

> *All hail to thee Mary*
> *Who savest from danger,*
> *And hail unto Him*
> *Who was born in a manger,*
> *How blessed the infant*
> *Who came as a stranger.*

Feast of Epiphany

The word 'epiphany' is a Greek word meaning 'to show' or 'reveal'. In the Gospel of Matthew we can read the account of the visit of the Magi or wise men to the infant Jesus bearing gifts of gold, frankincense and myrrh. The Church celebrates this feast on 6 January and it is the time when we put the three wise men into the crib.

Before the figures are put in the crib the following text could be used:

> Today is the festival of True Light as the star in the sky shows the three Kings where Jesus is laid in his manger. May the Spirit of God always guide us to find Christ in our lives and the lives of others.

As the three Kings are placed in the crib all present genuflect and say:

> Emmanuel! God is with us.

Scripture The sight of the star filled them with
Reading delight, and going into the house they
(Mt 2: saw the child with his mother Mary,
1-12) and falling to their knees they did him
homage. Then, opening their
treasures, they offered him gifts of
gold and frankincense and myrrh.

Closing Prayer

Hail Mary, full of grace,
The Lord is with thee.
Blessed art thou among women,
And blessed is the fruit of thy womb, Jesus.

Holy Mary, Mother of God.
Pray for us sinners,
Now and at the hour of our death. Amen.

Candlemas

On 2 February, forty days after his birth, Jesus is presented in the Temple according to Jewish tradition. At Mass, candles are lit by the faithful to remember the words of Simeon whose words are remembered by the Church in the *Nunc Dimitis* which is read in every Night Prayer of the Divine Office. The following is a special night prayer for the family for Candlemas night:

Opening Prayer

Lord, for years your people waited for their saviour, Jesus Christ. It is with joy that we welcome your Son into our family.

Alleluia!

Let heaven praise Yahweh:
Praise him, heavenly heights,
Praise him, all his angels,
Praise him, all his armies!

Praise him, sun and moon,
Praise him, shining stars,
Praise him, highest heavens,
And waters above the heavens! (Ps 48:1-5)

Scripture Reading (Lk 2: 22-28)

And when the day came for them to be purified in keeping with the Law of Moses, they took him up to Jerusalem to present him to the Lord – observing what is written in the Law of the Lord: every first born male must be consecrated to the Lord – and also to offer in sacrifice, in accordance with what is prescribed in the Law of the Lord, a pair of turtledoves or two young pigeons. Now in Jerusalem there was a man named Simeon. He was an upright and devout man; he looked forward to the restoration of Israel and the Holy Spirit rested on him. It had been revealed to him by the Holy Spirit that he would not see death until he had set eyes on the Christ of the Lord. Prompted by the Spirit he came to the Temple; and when the parents brought in the child Jesus to do for him what the Law required, he took him into his arms and blessed God; and he said: 'Now, Master, you can let your servant go in peace, just as you promised; because my eyes have seen your salvation which you have prepared for all the nations to see, a light to enlighten the Gentiles and the glory of your people Israel.'

Closing Prayer

In your mercy, Lord, dispel the darkness of this night.

Let your household so sleep in peace, that at the dawn of a new day they may, with joy, waken in your name. Through Christ our Lord. Amen.

Creating a
Sacred Space in
the Home

There is scarcely any proper use of material things which cannot thus be directed toward people's sanctification and the praise of God.

Sacrosanctum concilium 61

Much thought and effort goes into planning any home, yet often little or no thought is given to creating a place for sacred objects or a sacred space. It was traditional for Irish homes to provide a place for a sacred picture, statues, holy water or blessed palm. Often the kitchen was the focus for such objects as it was often regarded as the heart of the home, the place where people are nourished and tell their stories.

It can be difficult to maintain space for the sacred amid the hectic pace of modern life and a sacred space in the home can act as a place for peace, silence and meditation. It can also be viewed as a place of healing where photos of loved ones can be placed. Situations can be written about and placed in the area, and spiritual intentions can be sent from any person in the household for the healing, success and peace of all. This is a wonderful practice for children and teenagers to get involved in.

Nature has always been regarded as revelatory of the sacred and a walk by the seashore or through the forest can provide the basis for a place which is connected with the natural environment. Great enjoyment can be got from placing flowers, stones, sea shells, dried leaves and mosses in a decorative setting. Stones and bits and pieces can have a real significance if they are associated with places that are dear to us, like, for example, the original homestead or a walk or place that offers peace, quiet and reflection.

A sacred space can be created in any place in the house and it is best to allow your own imagination dictate the location and design. Whatever room you pick will benefit from the calm and prayerful presence that will be associated with the sacred place. Corners are particularly suitable as are bookshelves, tables and dressers. A decision can be made as to whether the sacred space will be a private sanctuary or easily viewed by visitors.

After natural elements are used, candles, icons, pictures, crosses, angels and oils can be placed in the space to create a spiritually uplifting atmosphere. There are no hard and fast rules as the sacred space should grow and unfold with you or your family's life. Prayers or lines from scripture or poetry can also be placed somewhere if they are of significance at a particular time. A font for holy water can be placed in the sacred space or near it.

Children take great pleasure in creating a sacred space. Be open to their creativity as it can be very inspirational at times. Children in particular bring colour and nature to a sacred space as they have little or no inhibitions about their creativity. Finally, take great enjoyment and pleasure from creating a place for the sacred in your home and in your life.